THE OTHER CHRISTMAS STORY

Written by
Lindi Masters

Illustrated by
Lizzie Masters

Published by

Written by©
Lindi Masters

Illustrated by©
Lizzie Masters

"THE OTHER CHRISTMAS STORY"
Copyright© 2018

Story written by Lindi Masters
Illustrated and Designed by Lizzie Masters

Thank you to IGNITE KIDZHUB© and all the kids from the UK, USA, South Africa and Australia for their artwork.
Special thanks to our mentors and friends Ian Clayton and Grant Mahoney, without whom we wouldn't have explored these realms.

This edition published by Seraph Creative in 2018©
www.seraphcreative.org

All rights reserved.© No part of this publication may be reproduced, stored in a retrieval system or transmitted, in any form or by any means, electronic, mechanical, photocopying, recording or otherwise, without the prior permission of the copyright holder.

ISBN 978-0-6399842-5-4

All rights reserved.© No part of this book, artwork included may be used or reproduced in any manner without the written permission of the publisher.

This Book Belongs to:
_____

It's Christmas time!

Judah excitedly jumped up and down on his bed.

"Judah, you need to get into bed so I can tell you a story!" said mom.

"Judah", said mom, "I want to tell you the real story about Christmas."

"This story is important because it is about how Yeshua came into the Earth."

"Even though Yeshua was the lamb slain before the foundation of the Worlds, He had to come to the Earth as man." said mom.

Judah settled down to hear the story.

Mary was a young girl who was born in Nazareth.

Mary came from the generation of King David and had served in the temple from a young age.

Mary was engaged to marry Joseph who was also from the House of David.

Angel Gabriel was sent by God to Mary and he said, "Rejoice highly favoured one. The Lord is with you, do not be afraid for you have found favour with God."

"Behold you will conceive in your womb and bring forth a son, and shall call His name Jesus."

"How can this be, I am not married?" said Mary.

Angel Gabriel told Mary that she was
pregnant because the Holy Spirit
had overshadowed her.

"That Holy one, who is to be born,
will be called the Son of God."
Gabriel said.

Then Mary told Joseph she was pregnant
and because Joseph was a just man,
a Tekton, someone who is wise and a
worker of sacred geometry and mysteries;
he was not going to expose Mary
and was going to keep it a secret.

An Angel of the Lord appeared to Joseph in a dream and said, "Joseph, do not be afraid to take Mary as your wife. The baby within her has been conceived by the Holy Spirit. When he is born, you must call Him, Jesus."

A decree was sent out to all the world by Caesar Augustus that everyone had to register in their own city.

So Joseph took Mary who was nine months pregnant and went to Bethlehem.

When Joseph and Mary reached Bethlehem, there was no more room for them at any of the Inns because there were so many people in the city.

So they found what could have been a cave.

And there Jesus was born. They wrapped him in cloths and lay Him in the manger.

There were Shepherds or Watchers who were keeping watch over the flock of Israel by night, which is the time of engaging mysteries.

The Angel of the Lord appeared to them and the glory of the Lord shone around them.

The Angel of the Lord said, "do not be afraid, for I have good news for you."

He told them that the Messiah had been born in Bethlehem.

All the angels and heavenly hosts began praising God.

So when the Angel of the Lord left, the watchers went to Bethlehem and found Jesus wrapped in cloths, lying in a manger.

When they left they told everyone what they had seen and praised God.

Meanwhile...

When Jesus came from the Father, through the Mazzaroth, followed by His star, there were nine Magi that came through the East gate to Jerusalem.

As they traveled, they asked where the King of the Jews was, because they had seen His star and they had come to worship Him.

Herod was very worried, he called all the chief priests and scribes together. They told him the King of the Jews would be born in Bethlehem.

Herod secretly called the Magi to ask them when His star appeared.

He asked them to come back and tell him where the child was so that he could go and worship Him. But this was a dodgy deal.

The Magi followed His star until it came and stood over where the young child was.

When they came into the house, they saw the young child and they worshiped Him and gave Him many treasures.

They were warned in a dream not to go back to Herod and they left another way.

When the Magi had left, the Angel of the Lord spoke to Joseph in a dream. He told Joseph to take the young child and His mother and hurry off to Egypt and to stay there until he got word.

Herod was looking to destroy the young child!

Herod had all the male children killed under the age of two in and around Bethlehem because that was the period of time the Magi had told him that His star had appeared.

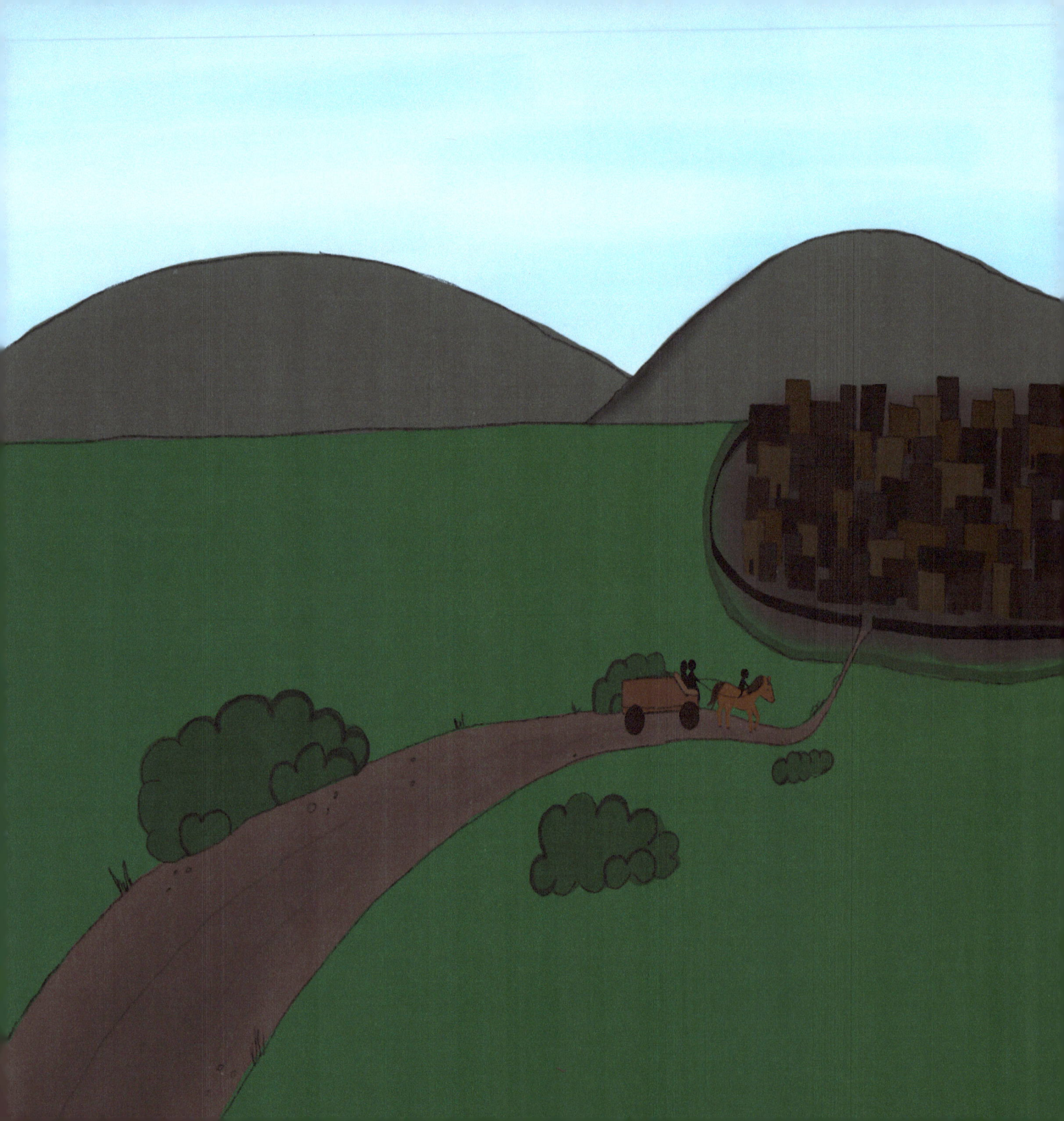

Much time later, Joseph was told by God in a dream to go back to Galilee and he came to the city of Nazareth.

And so continues
the amazing story of Yeshua,
the Son of God.

Judah settled down to sleep and dream in the mysteries of God that night.

He was so happy about the Christmas story and that Jesus had come to the earth to be our King and our Saviour.

"Goodnight Judah." said mom, as she closed the door.

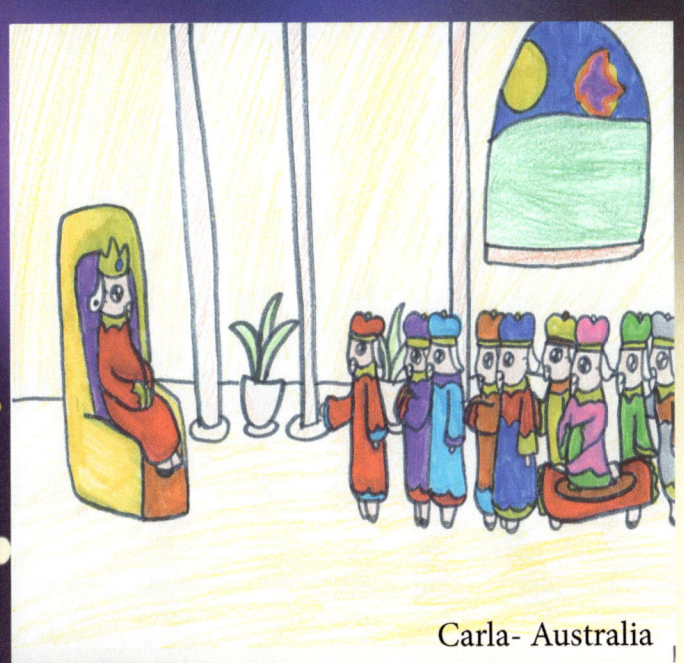
Carla- Australia

Joryn- USA

Jeiel- UK

Hannah- South Africa

Levi- South Africa

Luke- Australia

Roka- Hawaii

Reuben- UK

Locke- USA

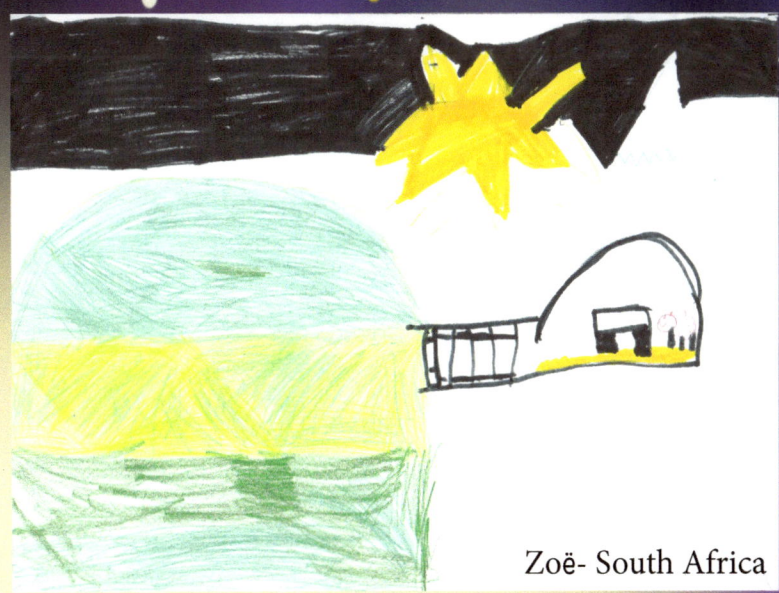

Zoë- South Africa

Carla- Australia

Reuel- UK

www.ingramcontent.com/pod-product-compliance
Lightning Source LLC
Chambersburg PA
CBHW041153290426

44108CB00002B/58